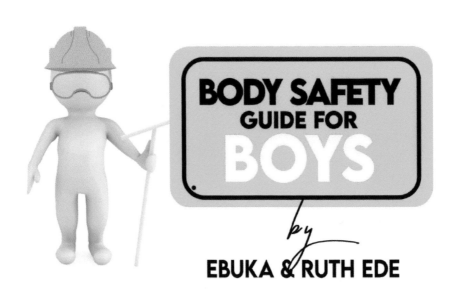

BODY SAFETY
GUIDE FOR
BOYS

by

EBUKA & RUTH EDE

Copyright © Ebuka & Ruth Ede

Save the Boys Initiative Boys Leadership Academy
08169877179 OR 08065649364 Savetheboysinfo@gmail.com, boychildacademy@gmail.com

First Published in 2023

Cover Design. Typesetting and Print Production
By: **HubTech.NG**
TechSupport, Printing & Publishing,
HQ DPPRS, Asokoro Abuja.
08115394079, (Whatsapp & Calls)

KEEPING MY BODY SAFE

JOIN ME ON THIS ADVENTURE

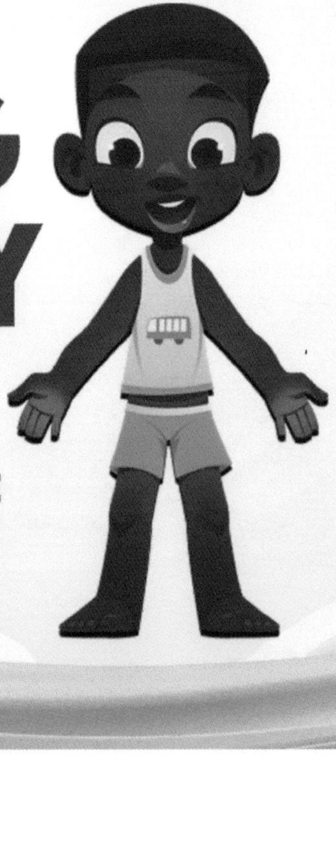

4

WHAT IS GENDER

GENDER IS THE QUALITY
OF BEING A BOY OR A GIRL.

I AM A BOY.

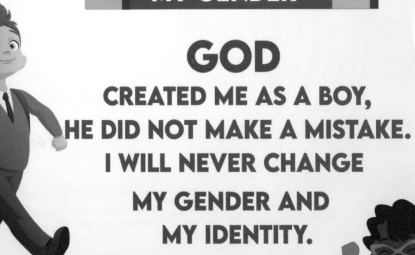

MY GENDER

GOD
CREATED ME AS A BOY,
HE DID NOT MAKE A MISTAKE.
I WILL NEVER CHANGE
MY GENDER AND
MY IDENTITY.

WHAT MAKES ME A BOY?

- ► I AM A BOY BECAUSE GOD MADE ME SO.

- ► I KNOW I AM A BOY BECAUSE MY BODY PARTS ARE DIFFERENT FROM THAT OF A GIRL.

- ► EVERY PART OF MY BODY IS SPECIAL.

MY BODY

EVERY PART OF MY
BODY IS PRIVATE TO ME.
THIS MEANS THEY BELONG
TO ME ALONE
AND
SHOULD NOT BE
EXPOSED.

SOME MAJOR PARTS OF MY BODY ARE:

▶ MY PENIS:

THIS IS UNDER MY PANTS. GOD GAVE ME PENIS TO URINATE.

GIRLS DON'T HAVE PENIS ONLY BOYS DO.

SOME MAJOR PARTS OF MY BODY ARE:

▶ MY BUTTOCKS:

GOD GAVE ME
MY BUTTOCKS
TO POO
AND
TO SIT DOWN.

SOME MAJOR PARTS OF MY BODY ARE:

▶ MY MOUTH:

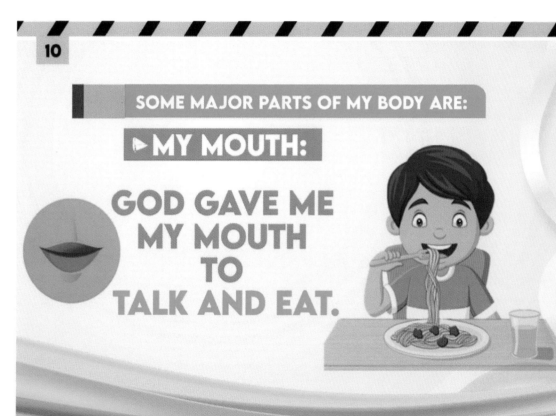

GOD GAVE ME MY MOUTH TO TALK AND EAT.

SOME MAJOR PARTS OF MY BODY ARE:

▶ MY NIPPLES (BREAST)

GOD
GAVE ME BREAST. IT IS MY PRIVACY, I WILL NOT ALLOW PEOPLE SEE IT OR TOUCH IT.

GOOD AND BAD IMAGE

A GOOD AND BAD IMAGE

GOOD IMAGE

A GOOD IMAGE IS ANY PICTURE, VIDEO, OR CONTENT THAT IS NOT HARMFUL TO YOUR MIND.

A BAD IMAGE IS ANY PICTURE, VIDEO, OR CONTENT THAT IS HARMFUL TO YOUR MIND.

BAD IMAGE

GOOD & BAD IMAGE

MY EYES ARE SPECIAL, IT IS NOT GOOD TO WATCH MOVIES, CARTOONS OR THINGS WITH BAD IMAGE.

THIS CAN AFFECT MY MIND IN A BAD WAY.

A GOOD AND BAD IMAGE

ANY PICTURE, VIDEO OR CONTENT THAT SHOWS A NAKED PERSON OR PEOPLE, SLEEPING, DANCING, TALKING OR PLAYING IS A BAD IMAGE.

THESE ALSO INCLUDES CARTOONS, GAMES, STORY-BOOKS, MOVIES AND ANIMATIONS.

BAD IMAGE

A GOOD AND BAD IMAGE

I MUST NOT ALLOW ANYBODY SHOW ME THEIR NAKED BODY OR FORCE ME TO SHOW THEM MINE.

I MUST STAY AWAY FROM ADULT PHONES, AND NOT ALLOW ANYONE SHOW ME BAD IMAGES ON THEIR DEVICES OR MATERIALS.

GOOD AND BAD TOUCH

GOOD AND BAD TOUCH

■ GOOD TOUCH IS SAFE TOUCH,
IT IS NOT ABUSIVE.

■ BAD TOUCH IS UNSAFE TOUCH,
IT IS ABUSIVE.

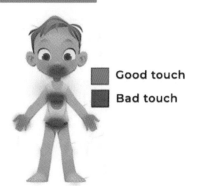

Good touch

Bad touch

EXAMPLES OF GOOD TOUCH

- HUG FROM PARENTS.

- A PAT ON THE BACK.

- SHAKING HANDS.

EXAMPLES OF BAD TOUCH:

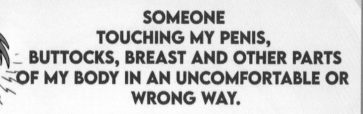

SOMEONE TOUCHING MY PENIS, BUTTOCKS, BREAST AND OTHER PARTS OF MY BODY IN AN UNCOMFORTABLE OR WRONG WAY.

GOOD & BAD TOUCH

- MY HANDS ARE VERY SPECIAL.
IT IS BAD FOR ME TO TOUCH ANOTHER PERSON'S BODY PARTS WITH MY HANDS.

- MY MOUTH IS A VERY SPECIAL PART OF MY BODY, IT SHOULD NOT BE USED TO KISS ANYONE OR ALLOW ANYONE TO KISS ME BECAUSE IT IS BAD.

GOOD & BAD TOUCH

- MY PENIS IS NOT A TOY FOR ME OR ANYONE, IT SHOULD NOT BE PLAYED WITH.

- IT SHOULD NOT BE TOUCHED BY ANYONE, EXCEPT FOR MEDICAL REASONS BY A DOCTOR AND WHEN MY PARENT ARE BATHING ME.

IF ANYONE TRIES TO
TOUCH ME IN A BAD WAY
OR FORCE ME TO TOUCH THEM
OR DO ANYTHING IN A BAD,
OR WRONG WAY.

I MUST REFUSE BY DOING
THE FOLLOWING:

WHAT I MUST DO IS:

HELP!!!

SCREAM AND CALL OUT FOR HELP!

WHAT I MUST DO IS:

**RUN AWAY
TO A SAFE PLACE
OR A
TRUSTED ADULT**

WHAT I MUST DO IS:

REPORT TO DADDY, MUMMY OR ANY ADULT THAT LOVES AND FEARS GOD.

WHAT WILL HAPPEN?
IF I DON'T REPORT

WHAT WILL HAPPEN IF I DON'T REPORT

THE PERSON WILL DO BAD THINGS TO ME THAT CAN MAKE ME SAD AND CRY.

WHAT WILL HAPPEN IF I DON'T REPORT

THE PERSON CAN HURT MY BODY WHICH CAN MAKE ME SICK.

WHAT WILL HAPPEN IF I DON'T REPORT

IT CAN MAKE ME TO
BECOME A BAD PERSON
IN THE FUTURE AND
AFFECT MY LIFE
IN A BAD WAY.

WHAT WILL HAPPEN IF I DON'T REPORT

IT CAN MAKE ME LOSE MY IDENTITY AS A **BOY.**

COMMITMENT TO PURITY

GOD MADE ME A BOY,
I WILL NEVER TRY TO BE A GIRL.

MY BODY IS FOR GOD.
I WILL NOT USE IT TO
ENGAGE IN ANYTHING BAD.

34

COMMITMENT TO PURITY

I WILL RESPECT OTHER PEOPLE'S BODY
(BOYS, GIRLS, MEN AND WOMEN)
AND WILL NOT ENGAGE IN ANY FORM
OF TOUCH OR ACTIVITY
THAT IS NOT GOOD.

I WILL SPEAK OUT, IF ANYONE TRIES
TO FORCE ME TO DO BAD THINGS

CONCLUSION

BE WATCHFUL.

BE CAREFUL OF WHERE YOU GO AND WHO YOU STAY WITH.

TALK TO YOUR PARENTS IF ANY OF THESE THINGS WE DISCUSSED HAS HAPPENED TO YOU.

THANK YOU FOR JOINING ME ON THIS ADVENTURE.

NOTES

_____

_____

_____

_____

_____

_____

_____

_____

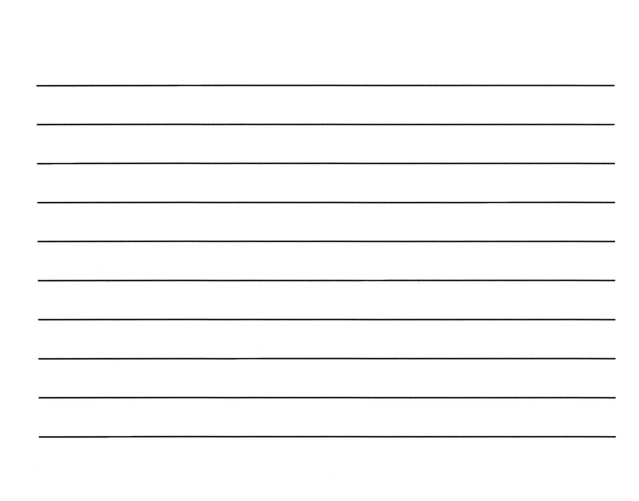

Printed in Great Britain
by Amazon

36804152R00025